I AM AMAZING GRACE

A Journey of Miracles Through Cancer

Grace A. Armstrong

I Am Amazing Grace: A Journey of Miracles Through Cancer
Copyright © 2024, by Grace A. Armstrong

ISBN: 979-8-9866703-9-3
Published by: SIP Publications, LLC
Printed in the United States of America

Edited by: Grace A. Armstrong
Cover Art: 5.13 Graphics & Media LLC

All real-life anecdotes are told with permission from actual parties involved and recorded to the best of the author's recollection. Names in some instances have not been used at the request of the individuals referenced. In some cases, parties mentioned are deceased. Details of some instances have been slightly modified to enhance readability, or to ensure privacy. Any resemblance of any other parties is purely coincidental.

All rights reserved. No part of this book may be reproduced or transmitted in any form electronic, or mechanical, including photocopying and recording, or held in any information storage and retrieval system without permission in writing from the author and publisher.

Scripture quotations marked (NLT) are taken from the Holy Bible, New Living Translation, copyright ©1996, 2004, 2015 by Tyndale House Foundation. Used by permission of Tyndale House Publishers, Carol Stream, Illinois 60188. All rights reserved.

Scripture quotations from The Authorized (King James) Version. Rights in the Authorized Version in the United Kingdom are vested in the Crown. Reproduced by permission of the Crown's patentee, Cambridge University Press

Advanced Praise for
I am Amazing Grace

Grace's journey under our pastoral care has been nothing short of inspiring. Her life and testimony vividly reflect the transformative power of God's grace. In sharing her story, Grace has become a beacon of hope and encouragement to those around her, including ourselves.

We are thrilled for readers to embark on her journey through these pages, confident that they too will be touched, uplifted, and enlightened by her unwavering faith and the profound impact of God's grace in her life.

~Pastor David and Lady Kelsey,
Christ Tabernacle Apostolic Church

"My most beloved mentor and friend introduced me to Grace. The first thing I remember was her kind smile, laugh and her love and respect for those caring for her.

Grace has shown me that the manner in which one lives through their cancer journey is one of the most important parts in beating it. This book stands as that testament. Please enjoy this authentic insight into Grace's journey; it is sure to benefit anyone who has been touched by cancer."

-Michelle Buerschen, CNP

DEDICATION

This book is dedicated to my readers.

I pray this book will be a guide for you when you are going through a difficult time. Just remember like the song says, God is a way maker, a miracle worker, a promise keeper, and a light in the darkness.

Never give up, and always have faith over fear.

CONTENTS

My Name is Grace 1
Hello Motherhood 8
Matters of the Heart 18
Life Changing News 22
Prayer Closet 29
Rededication, 2019 34
I'm, Okay, But I'm Not Okay 40
Faith Over Fear 45
Praying Through It 53
HEALING 56
There Is More 65
Getting To More 71
There Is Life After Cancer - It Is A Miracle 76
APPENDIX 1 78
APPENDIX 2 83
APPENDIX 3 86

FOREWORD

Cancer is no respecter of persons. Cancer, unfortunately, does not practice discrimination.

Throughout my 17 years of being a registered nurse, I have seen persons of all ages, races, religious affiliations, and socioeconomic statuses affected by cancer. I have seen people throughout the various stages of the cancer journey; from diagnosis to treatment, the medical and surgical healing aftermath, the celebration of remission and life renewed, and sometimes, regrettably, the journey to end of life. The cancer journey is a grueling quest filled with unexpected twists and turns.

I Am Amazing Grace: A Journey of Miracles Through Cancer, is an intimate look into the cancer journey of Grace Armstrong and shares the turbulent voyage through life with a cancer diagnosis, as well as the miraculous encounters experienced throughout a lifetime of growing faith.

I met Grace in 2020. It began with, what I thought at the time, a random Facebook post in our local town Facebook group asking if anyone needed childcare. I was pregnant with my fourth son and needed a smaller learning environment for my second son due to developmental, neuro-sensory and behavioral challenges he was having in traditional kindergarten. Under her support and guidance at her home-based childcare program, my son began to flourish. All my other boys have since attended her programs.

While I was a daycare parent, I learned that Grace was a cancer survivor. God placed me close to her and our relationship grew stronger when it was most needed. God showed me Grace's heart and helped me create a space to allow her to be who God intended her to be. God was speaking to me, and I was simply being obedient. We all need freedom to experience our emotions and live life authentically with love, support, and compassion. As a caregiver, sister-friend, or loved one of a cancer survivor, you get that same opportunity to create that space for loving, living, and healing.

This book is a must read for all those affected by cancer or another life-altering illness, and their loved ones/caregivers. This is not just Grace's story of faith-building through breast cancer. This is a full-spectrum cancer companion guide for everyone on the cancer and caregiving journey. Come along with Grace, as she recounts her cancer journey, offering inspiration and practical ways to exercise faith over fear. There are even resources for loved ones to assist with that remarkable/special caregiving journey. As I said before, the cancer journey is grueling. No matter what role you are playing in the cancer journey, this book offers insight into various parts of the experience which in turn will better equip you to be a part of the cancer-support network/tribe. This book gives an inside look at the hardships while offering inspiration to become a faith-filled overcomer!

Dive into Grace's first-hand account of her tumultuous cancer journey. I pray as you read Grace's story, you are able to see God's miracles at work in your own life. I hope that God speaks to you, renews your hope, love and most importantly, your faith. Lastly, I am wishing all of you strength to travail through the cancer journey.

                    LeAnnette Magba-Kamara, RN, BSN

I Am Amazing Grace
A Journey of Miracles Through Cancer

Grace A. Armstrong

For it is by grace you have been saved, through faith—and this is not from yourselves, it is the gift of God—not by works,
so that no one can boast.

Ephesians 2:8-9

"The miracles are countless."

~Grace A. Armstrong

MY NAME IS GRACE

Having breast cancer changed my life, but life before cancer wasn't always easy, either . . .

***

Growing up, my mother would speak in passing about how I was born several weeks prematurely. She mentioned to someone that my hair was shaved to insert tubes and needles and that I had jaundice. For a few days, I had to stay in the neonatal intensive care unit (NICU). Apparently, the doctors told her that I was supposed to die after three days.

I see the correlation of John 2:19 to the part of my life: *Jesus answered and said unto them, Destroy this temple, and in three days I will raise it up (KJV)*. There was biblical significance to three days. The doctors and nurses called me a "miracle baby" because they were surprised I lived beyond those three days.

It is because of God's hand on my life that I have been able to thrive. The miracles are countless. I wrote this poem to announce my birth. Knowing what I know about myself now, this is what I would have wanted my birth announcement to say:

Move Over, Find Space, Dance for Grace
(My Birth Song)

Move over, find a space and dance for Grace
She has favor, she is strong, she is brave, and she stands tall
Move over, find a space, and dance for Grace because she wakes, prays, and slays, every day
Move over, find a space to dance for Grace

Grace is beautiful
Grace is kind
Grace is gentle all around
Honestly, Grace is too much, but just enough for all of us

Move over, find a space, and dance for Grace
She has God's love and divine grace
Move over, find a space, shout out loud and
give God thanks as we dance for Grace

As my mother would say, "Move over and find a space the sun will shine upon your face as I, the Lord God has made you my Amazing Grace."

 I thank God for the fact that my mother was a praying woman. I know that she prayed when I was in her womb and as I grew up. Her prayers from 1973 continue to cover me even though she is now deceased. God saw fit that I would survive beyond those three days and my mother named me Grace.

I Am From Miracles

I was born and raised in the "Queen City," Cincinnati, Ohio, with my parents and two sisters. Early on, I developed my foundational belief in God, and I strongly believed in His power and love as a young child. My sisters and I were tight. We sang in church, and we believed we would be the next generation of the famous Clark sisters gospel group. I am grateful for the shared environment in our family household.

I loved to go swimming at the YMCA. In passing I used to see girls double dutch jumping rope in the gym. I would go into the gym and see what they were doing. One day I asked the girls, "What are you doing? Is this just for fun or are you competing?"

Several of the girls explained that they were trying to build a competitive team but needed a coach. "The woman who is helping us doesn't want to do it anymore." That intrigued me.

I told them, "Let me go home and ask my mom." To my surprise, she went to the Y and spoke to the director, who happened to be a close friend of hers. Mom agreed to be the coach and under her direction, I am proud to say that we won a national competition! I stayed with the Prancers for three years, through sixth grade. It became a family affair, mom formed teams for all age groups, so my sisters were able to compete too. Our first official team sponsor was a store where we bought candy from back in the day.

In middle school, I was a cheerleader and ran track. My love for doing hair was developed during that time. I used to do a lot of people's hair in the neighborhood. When I would babysit the little ones, I would make sure they went home with a fresh hairstyle. Much of what I do today as a daycare owner and cosmetologist was born in that time of my life.

Another time after swimming my right ear started to throb. I love to swim and one summer me and my sisters went swimming every day. I was screaming and crying because I was in so much pain. My mom took me to Children's Hospital and the diagnosis was "Swimmer's Ear." They prescribed some medication but my ear continued to hurt.

Mom called the doctor, and they sent me to an ear specialist who stuck an L-shaped instrument into my ear and sent me for X-rays. The scan showed that I had a blood clot in the middle of my ear. The doctor was concerned that the clot would move to my brain, so he recommended surgery.

By faith, my mother took me to a revival that night and testified about what was happening. I can remember her saying, "I believe that God is going to heal my child." The pastor was a well-known traveling evangelist. She called me up to the front of the church, where church elders and ministers surrounded me. The pastor anointed her hands with holy oil and stuck her finger in my ear. I can't remember what she prayed, but I do know that it was powerful for me.

At my next appointment I was supposed to be prepped for surgery, but there was no blood clot to be found. It was a miracle. This is how I came to strongly believe in God's power and love and His grace on my life.

"You are the God who performs miracles; you display your power among the peoples."

Psalm 77:14

"Whenever I feel nervous about getting things done, I face my fears with strength and bravery."

~Grace A. Armstrong

HELLO MOTHERHOOD

When I graduated from high school in June of 1991, I had a full ride to Wright State University. I was supposed to start college that August, but something told me I was pregnant. I delayed my starting date because I needed to confirm. I didn't go to college right out of high school, but I obtained my cosmetology license.

For a few weeks my mom and God mom had been asking me if I was pregnant. Because I began to gain weight, I kept denying it, but they found a way to get the truth.

If I could speak to my 18-year-old self, I would remind myself to be strong, stay authentic, and never stop loving myself. I would sit myself down and say, "Grace, you can do anything you put your mind to; dream big." I would tell my younger self, "Believe that you are capable of achieving anything you want in life."

The Set Up

I had spent the night at my grandmother's house and my mother called to let me know she and my godmother were on the way to take me to the mall to do a little shopping. I got ready, got into the car, and as we were driving, I noticed that we were not going to the mall. We ended up at a clinic and I asked, "Well, why are we here?"

They both said, "We're here to find out if you're pregnant, or not."

In the back of my mind, I was thinking, "Oh, they set me up to find out if I'm pregnant."

Once the nurse took me back into the examination room, my mom asked the nurse to give me a pregnancy test. As I was going down the hallway from taking the test, my mother peeked out the door and said, "I know she's pregnant. I know she is, just tell me, doctor, just tell me."

She said, "Miss Armstrong, you have to wait." I sat in the examination room with my mother and godmother. My mother said, "You know what? If you're pregnant, I just don't know what I'm gonna do. You'll be the first pregnant youth in the church."

I said, "Oh gosh."

The nurse came in and said, "Unfortunately," she paused, "You know, Grace is pregnant."

My godmother sighed, "Oh, Lord Jesus. What! She's pregnant?"

My mother said, "Can you check her? We need to find out how far along she is."

The nurse said, "Yes, we can check her. I have to go get the doctor."

As the nurse left the room, I sat on the table shaking. Out of the corner of my eye, I could see that my godmother was upset. She glared at me and enunciated the words, "I can't believe you are pregnant." They were both leaders in the church. "You are the first one pregnant in the youth group."

My mother was on the side saying, "Yes, get her for me too."

I offered, "Well, I can go to Chicago to my older sister's house, and I stay up there with my baby."

They said, "No. No, you're not doing that."

I said, "Well, I can just get an abortion."

My mom said, "No, you're not doing that either."

I'm sitting there trying to process the news. The nurse came in and let us know I was three months pregnant. My mother said, "After this, we're going to the house to set down and come up with a plan for you and this baby. Becoming a mother at a young age is not going to be easy Grace, but you will have support.

My Pregnancy

I was happy and nervous all at the same time to be pregnant. I had a lot of support from family and friends. Though it was embarrassing being the first youth in the church to be pregnant, I knew that my baby was a blessing.

In the beginning of my pregnancy, they thought I was having a miscarriage because I was spotting a little bit. After that, I didn't have any complications throughout my entire pregnancy.

When I had ultrasounds, the baby would never open their legs to let us know the gender.

Labor

The day I went into labor I was at my godmother's house. I woke up to my stomach hurting and the baby kicking, just moving crazy that day. I really didn't have an appetite, but because I had been laying around the house all day I got up to eat a sandwich. The sandwich made me nauseous so I laid down. After a few minutes it felt like I had to use the bathroom, and my water broke. My godmother called 911 and I was rushed to the hospital in an ambulance. She met me there.

They got me settled into a room and the nurse said, "We need to find out if your water really did break."

They checked me and she said, "Your water hasn't broken yet."

I said, "Ma'am, my water did break."

She kept saying that the machine didn't show it was broken. She got up and said, "Let me go get someone else." They checked me three times and my water had broken. The problem was that there was another sack up there that wasn't broken, and that's when I found out I was having twins.

I was in labor for 38 hours. The doctors had to induce my labor. During labor the baby kept crawling up into my pelvic bone. It felt like the baby was going up in my chest. The baby was distressed, and the heart rate was dropping so I had an emergency C-section. When they opened me up that's when they saw that my daughter was hovering over her brother.

Because of my anesthesia, I didn't know what happened during my birth until the next day. As the surgery was starting, the medication was wearing off. I kept saying, "I feel you cutting on me." Everybody in the room was looking around like, "What is she talking about?"

The doctor stopped making his incision, and said, "What did she say?"

The nurse says, "Doctor, she feels you cutting on her."

He said, "There is no way you should be feeling anything because of the medication, right? Tell me if you can feel this," and he started cutting again.

I screamed, "Yes!"

He said, "We need to give her more medication." They gave me so much that I went to sleep. I didn't get to see my son or hold him. I didn't even know that I had a little girl. Keisha was delivered first and she had a twin, my son, who didn't make it. Keisha was rushed to the NICU because she had a bowel movement inside of me that caused a small infection. I was discharged after a couple of days, but I had to leave my baby in the hospital for two weeks for monitoring.

After that pregnancy, 9 months later, I began to have a lot of pain in my abdomen, to where I had to go to the emergency room. During that visit they saw I had developed endometriosis and that I would need to have a surgical procedure called D&C. I had to have a lot of surgeries on my abdomen because I was getting tumors on my ovaries. Every six months I had to get a procedure called HSG where they put dye into my uterus and fallopian tubes, to show if my tubes are blocked or any abnormality in the shape of the uterus. This was allowing the doctors to see if I could have any more children. Unfortunately, the outcome was I couldn't have any more children.

I was a young woman, and the pregnancy was very difficult for me. I was traumatized because I did not understand what was going on with my body, nor did I understand the diagnosis. God saw to it to keep His hand on me through all my surgeries. It was a miracle.

We are all capable of changing when we need to. Now that I know how to treat myself better, I am being more intentional to make it a priority to practice self-care. I have developed healthy routines and priorities. Setting boundaries is not painless, but when I need to say "No" I will. It is a necessity for me to get adequate rest because a healthy mind is a healthy body.

Whenever I feel nervous about getting things done, I face my fears with strength and bravery. I recognize that life is too short to spend time with people who bring me down. I surround myself with prayer warriors, worshippers and loving people. I enjoy taking trips and doing new things. I love to laugh, and I do believe that laughter is the best medicine.

I enjoy taking my granddaughters to Kings Island amusement park. I love being with them, riding rides, and eating good food. Seeing the joy on their faces is priceless. If you know anything about Cincinnati, you know that people flock to our music festival every July from all over the country. Of course, I enjoy shopping and Kenwood mall is one of my favorite places to go. Eddie Merlot restaurant is one of my favorite spots.

One lesson I learned is that whatever you choose in life, whether good or bad, right or wrong, it comes with consequences. Although I had my daughter at a young age, LaKeisha is God's gift to me. Her name means Favorite, Great Joy, God is Gracious, Favor or Blessing. I have learned so much from her and she has given me my greatest gift—my grandchildren. God used what some may consider the "wrong" choice, one that people thought could have destroyed me, to get me to His divine destination of motherhood. At times it was challenging to be a single mother, but my daughter is my greatest joy.

*"She is clothed with
strength and dignity;
she can laugh at the days to come."*

Proverbs 31:25

"The condition of my heart needed to be repaired again."

~Grace A. Armstrong

MATTERS OF THE HEART

In 2010, I was preparing to celebrate the milestone of my daughter's high school graduation. At the time, there was nothing more important to me than seeing my child walk with confidence into the next phase of her life.

A couple of years later, in 2012, at a routine physical appointment, my life changed. The doctor checked my vitals and listened to my heart through the stethoscope. He asked, "Have you ever had like a heart murmur or had any problems with your heart?"

I shook my head and said, "No." I had no idea that I was having heart palpitations.

The doctor said, "Well, it sounds like you have a murmur. I need to get you over to the cardiologist just to be sure."

That was a scary and stressful time for me. I fell into a dark place because it felt like my world was caving in on me. I was in my thirties, and at the time, I sat down in the darkness of the unknown and let it consume me. The feelings of helplessness and sadness overwhelmed me. All the talk about heart disease and heart surgery made me worry that I was not going to live. I couldn't eat and I was afraid to go to sleep at night. The fear of dying in my sleep from having a heart attack was real after I had a heart attack and had to be hospitalized on the cardiology floor for seven days.

The doctor told me, "Your heart is beating too fast." I was required to wear a heart monitor for 30 days to check my heart activity. The results showed that the I had a short circuit. The official name for the diagnosis they gave me is Wollf-Parkinson-White Disease (WPW), which means that I had an irregular heartbeat.

On my maternal side of the family people had died young from having heart attacks, and my mom had congestive heart failure. Looking back, relating that time of my life to my walk with God, I was probably moving too fast causing my heart to race.

The first time I had heart surgery, the doctors performed an ablation. It was a 4-5 hour procedure where they went into my heart through the main artery in my groin. They spent two hours looking around and watching my heart. It was determined that it wasn't pumping the way they needed it to, so they spent another two hours trying to fix it by burning, freezing, or trying to correct it. After surgery, I had to lie flat on my back for 12 hours and be in UC hospital recovering for five days.

My second heart surgery was about a year later, in 2013. The condition of my heart needed to be repaired again; it was beating the opposite way. The doctors mentioned that I might need a pacemaker because the short circuit in my heart was precisely next to the natural pacemaker. I had to sign some papers and give my consent in case the bottom of my heart stopped, and I would need a pacemaker. Thank God that I didn't require one, I came through the surgery by

God's grace, and it was a miracle that I did not have to have a pacemaker.

Grace is a thread throughout my life.

"I'm going to be ok. Please, God, take the wheel."

~Grace A. Armstrong

LIFE CHANGING NEWS

During my annual visit to the gynecologist, in December of 2013, when she pressed on my breast, it was painful. My doctor said, "If it hurts, we don't need a mammogram, we have to take you straight to diagnostic testing." From that point on, it was a ripple effect of pictures, ultrasounds, and biopsies. Everything happened so quickly that my head was spinning.

In January of 2014, I had an appointment at the Women's Cancer Center to have a diagnostic test performed on my breasts. My breasts are dense which makes cancer hard to see on a normal mammogram. In the diagnostic exam, the machine gives the doctor a better view than a mammogram.

I changed into my gown, waited for the nurse to take me back, and afterward, she said, "Wait here."

I sat in the waiting room with my gown on. Three other women came in and I chatted with them as they waited to be examined. When the nurse came back she said, "Ms. Armstrong, the doctor needs more pictures."

I started to feel slightly concerned, but I followed her back into the examination room and had to go through the pain of the machine squeezing my breasts again. She took me back to the waiting room and said, "We need to wait for the results."

This was the third time I had to wait. At that point, I started to really worry and my mind started racing. I heard the nurse's feet hit the floor as she walked away. My heart was thumping hard in my chest and my hands began to sweat and shake. "Why do they need more pictures?" I thought. "What is happening?" I watched several women come and go. As I waited to hear my results, it felt like the wait for news took forever.

When the nurse finally returned, she spoke flatly, "Ms. Armstrong we have to do an ultrasound."

My heart dropped to the floor. I thought, "What did she just say? We still ain't done?" It was getting late, and I told myself, "Go to the lockers to get your phone." I had not told anyone that about the test. "Grace, call someone to come meet you," I thought. "Tell them what is going on." I just could not do it because I didn't want to cause alarm for anyone. I kept telling myself, "I'm going to be ok. Please, God, take the wheel."

I followed the nurse who took me to the ultrasound room. She just said, "Lay down on the table. I need to take some pictures before the doctor comes in." I laid back on the examination and looked through the window. I said to myself, "I cannot believe that this is taking place right now."

As the nurse began to do the ultrasound I started to softly sing "Great is Your Mercy," by Donnie McClurkin. Tears began to fall down my face and my body began to shake from fear and anxiety. I was so nervous that the nurse stopped the test and said, "I am done, but I need to go get the doctor." She stood up, "I will be right back to see what the doctor wants to do." She said, "You don't have to be scared, everything is going to be okay, but I understand. We have to have faith."

I began to pray, "God please give me peace and strength right now in the name of Jesus. Please, God, don't let this be bad."

A Cancer Diagnosis

The nurse returned with two doctors. They explained that they needed more pictures of my breasts. I laid there as they measured and took ultrasounds. When they completed the examination, one of the doctors said, "Ms. Armstrong, unfortunately, your images are showing a high possibility that you have cancer in your right breast. We will need to do a biopsy to confirm this."

I was so disturbed at the news that upon hearing the cancer diagnosis my ears shut down. The doctor was talking to me, but his words were going in one ear and out of the other. It felt like someone had taken a knife and stabbed it into my heart. I thank God for the nurse who was with me that day because she comforted me. She understood my emotions and my feelings and said, "It will be okay."

The only thing I remember one of the doctors saying is, "Ms. Armstrong we need to do a biopsy to confirm what we are seeing."

I don't remember how I had the strength to put my clothes on and drive home. I couldn't breathe while driving so I pulled over on the side of the road and called my aunt Robin who lived in Atlanta. As soon as I heard her voice on the phone, I lost it. My aunt said, "Gracie, what is going on? What happened?" It felt like I was having a heart attack because I was hyperventilating. I was sobbing so hard that I couldn't answer her.

There were no words to answer my aunt's question. What I know is that she immediately went into prayer, and I could hear her interceding on my behalf. As she prayed, I felt God's peace come over me and I calmed down enough to tell her through my tears, "I'm on my way home from the doctor. I had to pull over on the side of the road to call you." I took a deep breath, "The doctors just told me there is a high probability I have cancer in my right breast." I broke down in tears again.

My aunt said, "Gracie you know that God's got this, give it to Him and let Him work it out." As I cried, I heard her say, "Just believe that God will do it. You have to have faith. God will never leave you or forsake you."

I wiped my tears and at Aunt Robin's direction, began to take deep breaths and exhale slowly. I started the car and drove straight to my aunt Lorraine's house. When I told her what was happening, she said, "This is a lot."

I laid my head in her lap and allowed myself to feel my emotions while I was being loved. Aunt Lorraine spoke life into me and said, "Grace, I cannot see the now, I only can see what's going to happen at the end of the tunnel. I can see the light."

I said, "I know you can see the light, Aunt Raine but I'm not gonna make it to the light." I was so discouraged.

I was young and I had never had a mammogram. I had to have courage and endurance that came from a place, only God could provide. I was determined to beat the cancer and tackle it the same way I have every other obstacle in my life—with determination and the attitude, "I've got this! I can beat this!" The road ahead of me looked scary, but God provided support for me every step of the way, even when I didn't recognize it.

"Let us then with confidence draw near to the throne of grace, that we may receive mercy and find grace to help in time of need."

Hebrews 4:16

"As I began to release my fears in my prayer closet, God began to fill me with His spirit."

~Grace A. Armstrong

PRAYER CLOSET

When I got home, I went into my office which was also my prayer closet. I laid down on the floor face down and the scripture John 8:12 came to my mind:

> *Then spake Jesus again unto them, saying,*
> *I am the light of the world:*
> *he that followeth me shall not walk in darkness,*
> *but shall have the light of life.*

I prayed, "God you really have to help me. I can't think straight, and I have no words. My body is numb with shock. Where are You?"

I heard the scripture playing repeatedly and it began to comfort me. God was telling me to follow Him even though I was in the dark place. I didn't know how He was going to bring me to the light, but I yearned for the light of life. As I laid prostrate, I surrendered my fears to God and I heard Him say, "Grace, I understand my child, that it's too much for you. Sit back and allow me to take the wheel."

More scriptures came to my mind:
- I John 1:7
- Isaiah 55:9
- Proverbs 3:5-6
- Psalms 119:105

You have to believe that no matter how dark or difficult the path may seem, His light will always guide you to Him. As I began to release my fears in my prayer closet, God began to fill me with His spirit. I sat in my prayer closet and sang praises unto Him. I surrendered it all. I had to allow God to order my footsteps and guide me through. If you surrender to God, you will see the light at the end of the tunnel.

You don't have to stay in darkness when you fall into a dark place.

Exercising Faith

In February 2015, I had a biopsy of my right breast. LaKeisha had given me some words of comfort because I felt anxious before they called me back. She said, "Mom, it's going to be okay." She chose a song on her phone and began to play it for me. "God is with, Me. He has not given us the spirit of fear." She leaned over and put her arm around me. That calmed me until I had to go back for the exam and leave them.

I was scared and my heart was racing as I sat in the waiting room. I prayed, "God, I put my faith in you please be with me during the exam." A 20-minute exam turned into a 2-hour procedure. The doctor had to dig into my breast because the mass was deeper in my breast than what was expected.

The pain was unbearable, and I already have a low tolerance for pain. I asked him to stop the exam several times because I was in so much pain, but he could only stop once. The noise of the machine and the pain were so traumatizing for me. I said to myself, "I will never do this again in life!"

> *"God, I put my faith in you please be with me."*

A few weeks later I returned to the doctor, and I knew in my heart that the results were not going to be good. I braced myself for the news and she confirmed it. She was apologetic and had a strong bedside manner, but I began to cry. The doctor said, "We need to remove it surgically, Ms. Armstrong."

About six months later I had a lumpectomy on my right breast. They had to remove a metal clip where they had marked where the mass was. Going to the hospital for any reason was hard already, but being there for major surgery made it worse. My mom, LaKeisha, a cousin, a friend, and my granddaughter stayed with me through the check in process.

As the nurse walked me back to the dressing room, I began to sing songs of worship to myself. They let LaKeisha come back to see me before I had to go under anesthesia. I guess she could sense how scared I was, so she sat in the chair and started to play worship music from her phone. The music calmed me, and I felt the peace of God and His presence in the prep room.

*"Trust in the L*ORD *with all thine heart; and lean not unto thine own understanding. In all thy ways acknowledge him, and He shall direct thy paths."*

Proverbs 3:5-6

Thanks be to God; I woke up from the surgery–another miracle.

~Grace A. Armstrong

REDEDICATION 2019

It was a Saturday afternoon in December 2018, that I began to reflect on all the things that had happened in my life, and I realized I needed a fresh start. I needed to be cleansed of all the pain, turmoil, confusion, and hurt from everything I had experienced over the last few years. So, I made a commitment to rededicate my life and get baptized on January 6th, 2019.

I fasted for a few days before my baptism, praying and asking God to heal my body completely. For four years, I was diagnosed with several ailments and had several major surgeries. I needed a touch from God. I believed that when I went down in the water and came back up, I was going to be healed from the top of my head down to my feet. I stood on that firm belief.

The Pink Heart

When the doctor walked in, she greeted me, "Hi Grace. How are you? I am Dr. Reyna. I looked at your results and we will need to do an MRI with contrast as soon as possible." I looked at her quizzically and she said, "The contrast will light up your body to tell us what stage of cancer you are in."

I was dumbfounded. I asked, "What do you mean? Do I have cancer again?"

"Yes." Dr. Reyna continued, "In the meantime, I need you to get a genetic test to see what your family carries." I could not think straight, nor did I know what to say at that moment. I broke down so badly that they had to have a social worker come in to help calm me down.

Dr. Reyna said, "Grace, you can get dressed. I will be right back."

When Dr. Reyna came back into the room, she asked, "Are you ok?" I nodded. She reached into her pocket and placed a beautiful, pink heart into my hand. "This is a heart of faith," she said. "I want you to carry this heart with you every day." I carried that heart every day of my cancer experience, and it is still a part of me today. She told me, "Always keep your pink heart with you every day. I promise to be with you through this process."

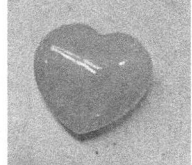

God sent Dr. Reyna to be in my life. I had never met a caring and loving doctor. She was there to help me get through the journey of cancer. We built a close relationship, and she learned so much about me that she could read me like a book. Every time I had an appointment and if there was a lot of information that she had to tell me, she would always say, "I know this is going to be a lot, but just tell me to stop when it begins to be too much for you to take in."

Dr. Reyna knew I would shut down if the information was too heavy for me. She would say every time, "Grace, ok, you just left me. You are not here with me, are you ok?" I would nod my head.

She would say, "No, I don't think so. Grace, I need you to breathe and relax for a few minutes. I need you to come back to me. Grace, it's ok and I do understand that this is a lot for you to take in by yourself. I promise that I will be with you to the end. I will walk this journey right by your side. I will do my best to help you understand this process as we go along." I was glad she finished the journey with me as she promised. We both cried when she moved on to another state to better her career. Dr. Reyna is still a part of my family.

A few weeks later, in February of 2019, I had another checkup with my doctor. As I walked into the OBGYN alone, my emotions began to rise in my chest. I prayed, "God, I cannot do this again." I cried, "This just may kill me." At that appointment I had to have a biopsy of my ovaries.

When I went back for the results, I was diagnosed with ovarian cancer. Two cancers at once! How was I to do this journey now that there is more going on? I was shocked when the doctor informed me, I had ovarian cancer. "You will need surgery to have a full hysterectomy."

Later that day I found out from the genetic test that I was a carrier for breast and ovarian cancer and that meant my daughter, who was in her twenties at the time, and her two young daughters must be proactive about their breast care and cancer prevention because they are at a high risk of getting cancer. Prior to the genetic test, I had no knowledge of breast cancer in my family.

Bad news just piled on top of me. I was overtaken with grief. I felt lost, helpless, broken, and alone with this news. I knew that playing the "Strong Black Woman" wasn't the answer, I had to be consistent with my medical appointments and encourage others to do the same.

Double Breast Cancer

On April 18, 2019, I had an MRI on both of my breasts. It was disheartening when the doctor felt lumps in both breasts. My emotions were all over the place, but I heard something say to me, "I got you." I was prescribed 18 pills to prevent an allergic reaction to the color contrast dye. They started an IV and I had informed my doctor that I believed I was allergic to the dye.

During the procedure, they put dye into my IV and my body went into anaphylaxis and cardiac arrest because of the dye. When I woke up, I was in the trauma room at the hospital with all types of tube and IVs hooked to my body. I could see that my daughter and best friend were upset. One of them said, "I don't understand what just happened."

Thanks be to God; I woke up from the medical procedure- another miracle.

Weeks after recovering from that debacle, I went back to see my breast surgeon. The news I got at the appointment was devastating, "You need a double mastectomy and a full hysterectomy." That news made me break down and they had to call in a social worker to calm me down. I could not think straight or feel my body. Going through that process was difficult. I know that God had His hand on me.

I had to stand on God's Word so I wouldn't lose my faith or get discouraged.

~Grace A. Armstrong

I'M, OKAY, BUT I'M NOT OKAY

At a doctor's appointment, I was informed that the insurance company was not going to cover my surgical procedures. I was told I would have to wait 30 to 60 days before they could do anything. That left me feeling insecure about the future.

"What will happen to me?" I thought. "Will I die before the doctors can do anything else?" I started to pray, "This is crazy, God. I am young and don't have anything together for my daughter or for my granddaughters." I said to myself, "If I die before this insurance kicks in, I need to make sure that my daughter is not left here doing this funeral planning by herself."

After the doctor's appointment, I drove straight to the funeral home. I walked into the building crying inconsolably. A woman who worked there greeted me at the door and asked, "Are you by yourself?"

"Yes," I responded through tears. The woman led me into a room, and we started to talk. After a few minutes, I started to calm down. I shared with her what was going on in my life and she began to help me start my pre-planning for my funeral. I almost always attended doctor's appointments solo. I had no group of sisters beside me, biological or spiritual.

I drove home from that meeting, fell on my bed and cried. I prayed, "Lord what is going on? Is this how I am going to die? I don't know what to do." I turned on worship music to calm my mind. After my nap I sent a text message to my family: "I need everyone to come to my house tonight for an emergency family meeting."

When everyone arrived, I had to tell them about the possibility that the insurance wouldn't cover my surgery. Then I told them that I went to the funeral home. The room got quiet and someone said, "You mean to tell me you did that by yourself?"

Questions were fired at me from all over the room, "Why would you do that? Did you know you didn't have to do that by yourself?"

I remember saying, "Well I did," and I handed them the funeral packet. "Here is the folder with all the information in it." My daughter was in shock.

It was hard to see how my family was reacting, but I had to stand on God's Word so I wouldn't lose my faith or get discouraged.

Major Surgery

On May 15, 2019, I had to go in for my full hysterectomy to address the cervical cancer diagnosis. The surgery went well, however during recovery I had a bad reaction to some medicine and had to stay in the hospital for seven days. My recovery at home was the worst thing ever; Recovery was dark and dismal. I fluctuated between levels of consciousness as I medicated myself for the pain. I was thrown into a whirlwind of hormonal imbalance due to not being able to take hormone replacement with breast cancer still in my body.

I didn't know that I needed to tell anyone how I was feeling. I felt like if I told someone they would just say, "You will be okay." Or "You are so strong." I didn't want to hear any of that. Nor did I want to hear, "Only the bravest and strongest of warriors were given this battle and difficult roads can lead to a beautiful destination." I wanted to cover my ears during some conversations.

Who would have thought that Grace would be fighting the cancer beast? Even if I had considered having a double mastectomy, the cancer could return. I didn't know if I had done something wrong to deserve what was happening to me, or if it was in God's plan. It's safe to say that I would not be the person I am today without undergoing "the beast." I thought, "This truly has to be a bad dream."

Recovery after ovarian cancer took me into medical menopause.

Fear not, for I am with you: be not dismayed, for I am your god: I will strengthen you, I will help you, I will uphold you with my righteousness.

Isaiah 41:10

"When fear knocks, let faith answer the door."

~Grace A. Armstrong

FAITH OVER FEAR

Although I was experiencing a hard time, God never left my side. I recall a time when Alaya, my oldest grandbaby, laid her hand on my chest and began to pray for me. Her young faith restored my faith. LaKeisha was also a pillar of strength for me:

My experience with my mom and her cancer journey was kind of unexplainable. I am not very good at keeping my emotions together, especially when it comes to her. I honestly believe that this situation helped me to increase my faith.

There were times where I had to hold it together so that my mom could fall apart. I tried to always stay positive and help her stay positive. I never let her see me fall apart; I was silent or leaning on my husband. One thing never changed; I believed that God would heal my mom according to her faith.

As believers we have to keep at our forefront that God has the final say, that is what I stood on. Some days were harder than others, but every time got easier because I believed that God would do what He said.

My daughter showed a strength that impressed me. For her, I continued to fight for my healing. I needed my grandbabies and my daughter to see me conquering my fear. I worshipped God throughout the journey –that is where my strength came from. I stood on God's promises for healing and strength; He did not let me down.

Do Not Fight Alone

I went to every doctor's appointment by myself. I felt, "I am strong, I don't need anybody to go with me." To this day, I wish I would have had someone to go with me instead of thinking, "I don't want to put this on anybody's plate."

There were plenty of times that I had breakdowns in the doctor's office, and they had to call a social worker to calm me down. If I had been with someone, they may have been able to help me understand what the doctor was saying before I internalized it in a way that they did not intend. I did not always understand the medical terminology or the side effects of the medication they were giving me.

Cancer is bigger than you. You need a support team, and I encourage you to love yourself enough to make sure you get all the information that you need and take someone with you.

I can also see the enemy often sends a counterfeit to the genuine gift God has for you. I learned that not everyone who has agreed to come along on your journey will stay when it gets hard, inconvenient, or uncomfortable. Health issues like cancer have tested many types of my relationships. My sickness and that of my mother, changed everything I thought I knew about sisterhood. On this journey you need a tribe, a true sisterhood that doesn't just offer words but actions to support you.

From 2015 through 2021, I had a sister-friend who walked the journey off and on with me. When I asked her to reflect on the experience, I was brought to a place of gratitude for her presence with me during that time:

Can you imagine going to pick your son up from the childcare provider and notice that something isn't right? Well, this is how my journey walking with Grace and her family through her road to recovery from cancer began.

I took Grace to medical appointments, and in September 2015, I took her to surgery. We laughed, cried, prayed, and believed together that all things would work out. We trusted God that there would be no lack in Grace's life. The experience allowed me to realize the true importance of genuine relationships.

Cancer is one thing and breast cancer is another. Despite it all, Grace came out as Amazing Grace.

Sister do not skip your medical appointments. Go to the doctor often and with intention. If you need support, have a friend or family member go with you. You are not alone, someone is always in your corner, ready to support you.

Advocate for Yourself

One thing that I learned during my cancer journey is how to speak up for myself. I had one nurse who made me feel like I was bothering her when I asked questions. It felt like she was thinking, "I just need her to shut up and let me do what I do."

As my own advocate, I was able to create allies that looked out for me. I have heard stories about how medical professionals have brushed women's concerns off, dismissed them, and ignored them, especially because of the kind of insurance they had, or because of the color of their skin.

Unfortunately, there are some women who have gone to doctors to raise concerns but were ignored.
When they returned after the situation worsened to Stage III or IV, they were told, "There is nothing we can do, you are now in an advanced stage of cancer." Those experiences taught me the importance of self-advocacy and consistent medical checkups.

You know your body better than anybody, speak up for yourself when something hurts, if you feel uncomfortable, and when something feels abnormal. I didn't leave my medical appointments until they told me, and I understood what was going on. I refused to be ignored, overlooked or minimized in my appointments. I thank God for the caring team of professionals along my medical path and I thank God for the grace of early detection of my cancer.

Conquer Your Fear

You must stay in the word and pray in order to conquer your fear. Learn how to trust God, no matter what you face. He promised to never leave you or forsake you. If you stand on His Word, God will lead you to the light. God has given us a promise of strength:

You armed me with strength for battle; you humbled my adversaries before me.

Psalm 18:39

Cancer picked the wrong diva to mess with. Fighting it takes everything you have. The best way to fight it is to take it one day at a time. Resist the urge to take care of everyone around you and focus on yourself. You are stronger than you think.

Feeling Overwhelmed

In July 2019 I started seeing various of doctors, surgical teams, breast specialists and hematologists—all working with me to plan and manage cancer in both breasts. You may feel overwhelmed, too, but know that with God, things will be a little easier. You are not alone. As a sister in the fight, I love and care about you and what you are going through.

I used to waste a lot of my life worrying. Utilizing faith is a life skill that I developed and became good at. Through this journey I have found that with a little practice, and a little patience, I can overcome fear with faith. I have chosen to be guided by God's promises instead of worrying about things beyond my control. This has allowed me to live a fuller, happier life.

No matter what life has thrown at you in the past, you have survived it. Hold on to your faith so that you can beat cancer, too. Fear can be a burden for us as cancer survivors.

The fear of pain, death, financial strain, and all the other unknowns are common concerns we face. I am asking Jesus to renew your heart and mind with holy and good thoughts as you're filled with the comfort and strength of the Holy Spirit.

Face fear head on and conquer it with your faith in Jesus Christ. Remember, you can always have faith over fear. God has not given us the spirit of fear, but he has given us the spirit of a sound mind. I have learned that our lives move in the direction of our strongest thoughts.

He hath put my brethren far from me and mine acquaintance are verily estranged from me my kinsfolk have failed and my familiar friends have forgotten me.

Job 19:13-14

"A butterfly blessing is the small, almost unnoticeable feeling of God's comforting, reassuring presence."

~Grace A. Armstrong

PRAYING THROUGH IT

Four years after my first diagnosis, I received a diagnosis of cancer in my other breast. I had a group of spiritual sisters who came together in July of 2019 to support me. I considered these women my "angels," because they committed to looking out for me and supporting me on my cancer and healing journey with prayers and other types of help.

On November 12, 2019, starting at 5:30 a.m. I had a double mastectomy with reconstruction. This procedure was scheduled for 13 to 16 hours. I was put into a medical coma and the doctors had to move blood vessels from my abdomen to my chest to keep my breasts alive. It was a miracle that I made it through that surgery.

When they were prepping me for my operation, I couldn't think straight. It required four needles in both breasts plus two epidurals in the upper part of my back. My daughter, LaKeisha, and goddaughter Jewel went with me to have the midline placed in my right arm the day before surgery. There were four different teams that had around 30 people on each team and two anesthesia teams in the operating room with me.

Preparing for the surgery was traumatic for me. I had to block out everything and mostly everyone to stay focused. Although I felt alone because of the cancer, my hope came from being a child of God. I prayed earnestly, "God, I trust you. I know that you can heal me."

LaKeisha and my youngest sister were with me at the pre-op appointment. I was so thankful that LaKeisha had the mind to ask the medical team specific questions. I saw her writing down everything the doctor said including the names of medications, and dosages to make sure she had everything right. Having them with me gave a different perspective and an advocacy that I didn't realize I was missing. Have someone at your appointment who is always willing to advocate for, and with you.

Even when the darkness covered my eyes I kept praying, "God I am asking you to help me." At one point I did get angry and I lashed out at Him, "How dare you do this to me? You gifted me with this gift and now you are taking away something that nurtures children." I felt like my womanhood was being stripped from me.

LaKeisha and I kept my "angels" updated with text messages and videos all day. She shared about my progress and what care was needed once I returned home. Despite the updates provided, the group texts started to slow until they eventually became silent.

I had a seven-day ICU stay because I could not maintain stable oxygen for three days. I didn't have many visitors, and it was disappointing for me that the promises so many people made were not fulfilled. I couldn't help but feel like their sentiments were "lip service."

"Thankfully I had women who stepped up for me and filled in the gap when I needed them."

~Grace A. Armstrong

HEALING

When I was discharged from the hospital Jewel volunteered to come care for me at my home. Although I was thankful for her, I didn't want to be a burden on a 21-year-old young adult. It disappointed me that the support I hoped and longed for from friends during my cancer journey quickly dissolved. Not everyone who joins your journey will remain with you until the end. People will make promises before God to pray, uplift, and support you. They will say that they will bear your burdens (Galatians 6:2), yet not everyone is able to walk the path with you. Thankfully I had women who stepped up for me and filled in the gap when I needed them.

Jewel stood in the gap for her "Mama Grace" and that blessed me. When the people who had offered to bring food, pray, visit, and rally around were strangely quiet, Jewel was right by my side. She helped me get dressed, gave me my medication, and assisted me with getting in and out of the car when I had to go to medical appointments.

I asked her to share what it was like for her when she was serving me:

When Momma Grace had her double mastectomy, I didn't know how to feel. I knew I wanted to be there to help and support her. I could tell that she was feeling anxious about being on restrictions for such a long period. I could see the effects of stress on her face. Because I was helping her, I realized that God had sent me to be at the house during her recovery. I was able to do things that she could not do for herself but needed done. I was raised to keep a clean house so it was easy to keep the house clean.

I remember one particular day when she was sitting in her recliner chair, and I was sitting on the floor next to her feet. I had my head on her knees as we watched TV. I felt so moved that God had placed me there, "for a time such as this," I thought about how Esther must have felt.

I thought, "It is a blessing to be with a powerful woman of God who has been diagnosed and been through this difficult surgery." The worries of Mama Grace's heart were growing so big that they spilled out into emotional moments. I was at her feet praying. I asked God to use me as a vessel and He placed me with Mama Grace, at her feet. I was honored to be by her side and do things she didn't want to ask anyone else to do. It brought me so much joy to help one of the strongest women I know at her weakest moments. She may not know it, but Momma Grace has blessed me in ways she may never know.

Through the ups and downs of life, I plan to be there whenever I can. My heart loves her to the moon and back. This spiritual mother-and-daughter union is blessed and inseparable.

A Spiritual Mother

My spiritual mother Ms. Harriett prayed and covered me in the spirit:

When Grace and I became closely acquainted in 2021 she educated me on her cancer survival journey. I also learned of her mother who was very ill and had been promoted to Glory shortly thereafter. Hearing Grace's story placed me in a state of AWE having a great deal of empathy and compassion for her. Seeing her walk through this challenging journey was the most amazing act of faithfulness I had ever seen. If you didn't know her story(s), you would never know the battles she was up against and what it took to maintain normalcy.

Through it all Grace continued singing and praising God for what He had already done, not to mention what He was about to do. The cancer returned and she was devastated. Only this time she had a sister circle of individuals to support her through another round of surgery and healing, along with God's promise: "And surely I am with you always, to the very end of age" (Matthew 28:20).

Once again through her faithfulness she put her trust in the Lord. God says: "Do not let your heart be troubled, nor let it be afraid" ...John 14:27.

To this very day, healing continues, but Grace has living faith the size of a mustard seed (Matthew 17:20). She is a living testimony, a Kingdom Winner, strong, courageous and faithful.

Restoration of Covenant Sisterhood

When I least expected it, covenant sisters were drawn to me. I met my sister-friend in the year 2020 when she brought her son to my childcare center. We began to build a friendship outside of the childcare services I provided. When my mother got sick and passed away our relationship grew closer. LeAnnette took out time to send encouraging text messages and scriptures that were laid on her heart such as:

- 1 Thessalonians 4:13-18, which encouraged me to have hope
- Jeremiah 29:11 speaks of God's thoughts of peace toward us and plans for a hopeful, prosperous future.
- Isaiah 61:3 reminded me that God will give me beauty for ashes.

LeAnnette had no idea that I was in a dark, lonely, and broken space when she sent those scriptures. Every time I had received a text message from her and read it, it was literally saving my life. I was feeling like I didn't have anyone to talk to that would allow me to express how I was feeling, and she was being obedient to God by sending a message or scripture, cards, flowers and support. LeAnnette was a Godsent, beautiful butterfly who represented hope, beauty, rebirth, endurance, freedom and love. Our relationship is built on and embodies all these things.

The symbolism of butterflies evokes the qualities of freedom, earthly beauty, love, and the human soul. With this butterfly being in my life, I began to feel and recognize God's blessings all around me. I have heard that a butterfly blessing is the small, almost unnoticeable feeling of God's comforting, reassuring presence. Through her, I realized that God had sent me the sister-friend I prayed for.

A genuine sister listens to God concerning her sisters. God still operates using the still, small voice that urges us to do acts of kindness, check-in, make that phone call, offer a listening ear, or stop by to determine if things are going okay. True sisterhood is an extension of the love of God that is able to be shared on a deep level. A true sister will display an unconditional love that remains constant even when you are feeling at your worst mentally, physically, or emotionally. The true sisterhood bond helps to heal wounds of the past and helps you to develop a deeper understanding of what love really is. In my covenant sisterhood, I find a genuine love and true appreciation for who I am, flaws and all.

Genuine sisterhood is sometimes composed of your "tribe"; your group of women that God places in your life, just for you. These sisters, mothers, and friends all come alongside you and become your shoulders to lean on and your biggest cheerleaders in life. Your success is their success. Sisters speak life into you. They are ready to pray for you and with you. My sisters aren't afraid to call heaven down or rebuke the devil on my behalf. Sisters are ready to offer both guidance and support. Offering spot-checking and direction to me as I go along my journey in life.

Proverbs 27:17 says, "Iron sharpens iron" and in a true covenant sisterhood, our sisters sharpen us and make us better people. My true sisters love me and are gentle with my spirit. Sisters have to be honest with each other, recognizing that no love is lost when we assist one another to navigate the hard, rocky places in life. My sisters never let me settle for less than I deserve, reminding me of who I am in God's eyes.

We have to forgive because we are human, but God gives us what is required to carry on. Sometimes my sisters remind me to celebrate the small wins in life and celebrate with me. Other times they offer a safe space to release my emotions and authentically be me. True sisterhood is present when you don't have the strength to move forward. A sister will hold you up physically and lift you up in prayer when your strength wavers.

I now clearly recognize genuine covenant sisterhood. God knew I needed true sisters/sisterhood despite the scars of my past. He heard my cries like Job: *"My friends scorned me: but mine eye poureth out tears unto God."* Job 16:20. He gave me the precious gift of sisters who are not just bound by having the same parents, church, or circumstances. God-given sisterhood is a response to my prayers.

A Prayer for Healing

Lord,

I entrust my life into your hands and ask for Your healing touch to be upon me.

May your love and grace be a source of comfort as I face this battle.

Amen

"There is more to grace."

~Grace A. Armstrong

THERE IS MORE

The stress and strain of sickness changed the dynamic of some of my relationships, including my sisterhood relationships. The loss of those relationships compounded by the fact that I couldn't lean on my biological sisters, caused me to need somewhere to feel safe.

My biological sisterhood suffered in 2021 when Momma took sick. Her sickness spanned from September 2021 through December 2021. Things continued to be strained in December 2021, when she was admitted into the hospital and 10 days later passed away.

After Momma's passing and funeral, the remnants of my biological sisterhood began to dissolve. The deep despair of processing multiple losses and battling health concerns left me in a tornado of emotions. God was the one who held me up.

After Momma passed, I tried to hold on to what was left of my sisterhood, both biological and spiritual. I reached out to my spiritual "family" however, reach back was slim to none. There were a few "spiritual sisters" that remained after Momma's passing. That is when God revealed that some people are only here for a short season of your life.

It was a depressing time of emotional confusion and sadness for me without sisterhood, or my mother. I'm thankful that God never leaves us or forsakes us. He calls us to lean on Him and place all our cares on Him because He cares for us (1 Peter 5:7).

I felt myself changing into a private person. I wasn't able to share any experiences with my biological sisters. This reality spilled over into my journey as I started to experience health issues again. I began to look for sisterhood and God revealed it in unlikely places.

While leaning on God and trusting Him, a spiritual transition was beginning. In the quiet solitude, God was preparing me for more. In December of 2022 I had surgery and while I was recovering, I couldn't do much for myself. I had a friend come help me, but five other women had rotated to help me. They had a rotation to stay overnight with me, give me my medication and help me around the house.

At the end of the year, I was disappointed that I couldn't go to church. After my mom died it was hard for me to sing praise and worship there. When I would get up to sing praise and worship, my heart felt like it was broken into a million pieces, and I did not know how I was going to be able to even utter the words. I felt such heaviness from grief. When I recovered from the surgery, God sent me to worship at a different church.

In January of 2023, the Lord began to restore things back to me. The recovery season was a quiet place for me. Through my prayer and worship, God began to reveal several specific steps for my life including opening a children's hair salon. I sat in my recliner listening to God and I asked, "How can I do this when I am recovering from surgery?" I was obedient and wrote down all of the steps.

In February of 2023, I was led to go visit another church. My granddaughters are on a dance team based out of Christ Tabernacle and come to find out their coach was my cousin Coach Kelsey. I was there so much due to picking up the girls from practice and meeting some of the members through the dance team. I started to feel God pushing on me to visit Christ Tabernacle, so I did. When I pulled into the church parking lot, I saw signs all around that said, "Love Lives Here". I kept asking the question to myself what that meant, because the love that I experienced hurt me. When I walk into the sanctuary, I began to understand why God sent me there. I soon found out exactly what that meant through the people and most of all God through them. That Sunday I received a word that was confirmation of all the things God was telling me to do, and the more was from my healing from a lot of things that had taken place in my life allowed me to be able to receive more. I joined Christ Tabernacle Apostolic Church in August of that year, under the leadership of Pastor David and Lady Kelsey Harding.

By May 13, 2023, I was hosting the grand opening of Kingdom's Kids Magical Hair Boutique. God showed me that He was preparing me for more and I had no idea that He was going to bless me in the way that He did. My healing process allowed me to be able to receive more.

It was another season of losing sister-friends, and being deceived by the enemy, but God did not allow any schisms to separate me from my daughter, from my healing or from God. At my new church God gave me peace of mind and He settled my heart. I have walked in my healing since the first day I entered the sanctuary of Christ Tabernacle. I had to experience all of that to understand that there is more to my story.

There is more for me to get to, and I have so much to give to others. I have more peace now. There is more to being amazing grace and God prepared me for what I am doing now. I never would have thought that I would be standing in my total healing. I feel so much better than I did during the dark years of 2019 through 2023. There is more to Grace.

Praise Is What I Do

I love to serve as a praise and worship leader at Christ Tabernacle. I get my strength from my worship, and I make time for quiet reflection each day. Being at my church has helped me to walk in my healing. The safety of my church home has helped me tremendously and I thank God for that favor on my life. As we say "Love Lives Here"

"He giveth power to the faint; and to them that have no might he increaseth strength."

Isaiah 40: 29

Four things to remember:

1. *God will make a way for you.*
2. *God is fighting your battles.*
3. *Prayer is the best medicine.*
4. *Trust in God's timing.*

~Grace A. Armstrong

GETTING TO MORE

"There is something you must always remember, you are braver than you believe, stronger than you seem, and smarter than you think."

~A.A. Milne

If there was one thing that I would say to another cancer patient and their family, it would be this quote from Winnie the Pooh. There is always hope behind what you see. It's possible not just to survive, but to thrive and to live a healthy and wonderful life again. Don't wait for life to change, live now.

Choose joy.

There are so many things about cancer that are beyond your control, but how you react is entirely up to you. You are in full control of your own attitude; cancer has no power over joy. Cancer cannot defeat your spirit.

> **"Cancer has no power over joy."**

Choose to be joyful and glad that you are alive. Lean into the Lord, put your trust in Him and never give up hope. There will be days as a survivor when this feels impossible. It is okay to be discouraged, but don't linger there. The way that you handle your circumstances shapes your character. Your cup is either half empty or half full. It is all in how you choose to see it. Don't let worry or fear steal your joy (Joshua 1:9).

I am inspired by my journey and the journey of other cancer warriors. There isn't a day that I do not think about cancer and how fortunate I am to be alive. After undergoing extensive chemo, radiation, and surgeries, I have come out on top. Today I am driven by the grace of God, my strength, and my support group who helped me fight and survive cancer. It saddens me to see other sisters battling this disease. My heart is with those who have won their victory on the other side.

Cancer has given me a different life than most women. There are harsh treatment issues that I will have to deal with for the rest of my life. I will live with lymphedema for the rest of my life. I go to survivor checkups, and I see men and women who are survivors. All of us are striving to keep cancer at bay, praying that we don't suffer from side effects of medications. It is a blessing to be a survivor.

God has given me joy and peace unspeakable. I often ponder Ephesians 3:20-21:

Now to Him who is able to do exceedingly abundantly above all that we ask or think, according to the power that works in us, to Him be glory in the church by Christ Jesus to all generations, forever and ever. Amen.

I have seen miracles performed. God has given me joy and peace unspeakable. My goal is to stand on a foundation of unshakeable faith by feeding myself with His Word each day. I know that faith without works is dead (James 2:17). God used a song by Elevation Worship entitled "More Than Able (He's Not Done With Me Yet) to help me to understand that there is more to my story. As the song says , "I still got joy in chaos, I've got peace that makes no sense."

Being confident of this very thing, that he which hath begun a good work in you will perform it until the day of Jesus Christ

Philippians 1:6 (KJV)

God has more for us than we can ever imagine. I learned to trust His plan. I now walk in the confidence that I am a powerful, anointed woman of God, because of the miracles. For that reason, I will always give back to women. I don't ever miss a chance to give my testimony – I want you to know that God has more for you, too.

This is my story—a journey of miracles through cancer. God has shown me throughout every challenging season in my life, that He is always there and that He wants the best for me. He reminds me that He wants to make my life a life of beauty. If He healed me three times, He can do anything but fail. God is not done with you yet.

I am praying for you,

A gift from me to you
Accept what is
Let go of what was

Have faith in what will be
Surround yourself with only people who are going to lift you up higher

Cancer is a word not a sentence

When you go through deep waters remember:
the Lord God will be with you.

The Golden Bell

This is the day I have been praying for.
Ringing the bell signifies a great accomplishment,
It means the end of a tough chapter of chemotherapy
and/or radiation and the beginning of a new one.

I ring the bell three times well, it's toll to clearly say,
"My treatment is done. This course is done and
I am on my way to a new chapter."

I ring this bell for myself and every other cancer patient
who has, or is, or will walk the journey that a cancer
diagnosis brings.

I ring this bell for my caregivers, family, friends, and
strangers who have given time, talent, prayers, and
encouragement on my behalf.

I ring this bell for each servant working within these
walls, thank you for the compassionate care
you chose to give daily.
I praise and thank God for you

I ring this bell.
I ring this bell.
I ring this bell on this day.

THERE IS LIFE AFTER CANCER - IT IS A MIRACLE

Thinking back on the surgeries, recoveries, setbacks, clinical trials, and life changing moments, allows me to recognize that I am grateful and blessed. I no longer take life for granted and value it more than I did before cancer. I have unshakeable faith over my fears and making the most of each day is important to me.

Fast forward eight years later, I am a kingdom winner, an entrepreneur, a mother, and a grandmother who stands stronger in the Lord. I say a daily affirmation and one that comes to mind for me to share with you is:

Blessed are those who trust in the Lord and have made the Lord their hope and confidence.

Jeremiah 17:7

I hope and pray that some of the changes that have enhanced my life will work for you as they have worked for me. My attitude changed in a more positive way when I learned and practiced the following:

1. I speak up when I need to be heard.
2. I pick my battles.
3. Get rid of negativity (people, things, ways of thinking).

When you have heard those awful cancer words you realize life is worth fighting for. Don't cloud your new life with negativity. Walk through your journey of miracles having God's grace.

You Are A Survivor

The day you were diagnosed you became a cancer survivor.

A survivor is someone who continues to live.

Think of survivorship as a mindset.
Each day is an event so do things that are meaningful to you.

Live in the present, do not focus on the past
or try to predict the future.

Cancer is a part of your story, but don't let it define you.

Delight in life and have faith that God's has a plan for you even if you can't see it now (Jeremiah 29:11).

APPENDIX 1

TIPS FOR CHILDREN COPING WITH A PARENT'S DIAGNOSIS OF CANCER

LaKeisha Hawthorne,
Grace's Daughter

LETTING THE DIAGNOSIS SETTLE IN

After hearing all of my mother's diagnoses, there was procedure after procedure and test after test. My days felt disrupted.

It came to a point that I shut down because of the news. My mom was diagnosed with not only cancer, but double breast cancer and ovarian cancer all at the same time. I remember at her first procedure I could see how scared and nervous she was about it. God laid it on my heart to play worship music to calm her down. I prayed that God would give her peace because my mom is a worshipper.

The first song I played for her was "Healing is Here" by Deluge. Then I played "Reckless Love" by Bethel Music and after that day a song list was born to help us get through that difficult season of our life.

A Child of a Parent with Cancer

Nothing felt normal to me after my mother's diagnosis. I have learned that the hardest thing for children of parents who have cancer is to come to terms with the fact that what they are experiencing is real. There are hundreds of different cancers with different outcomes, but some things remain the same. I felt so many different emotions and I was afraid people would treat me differently. It also terrified me to say out loud, "My mom has cancer," because after that it will be real to me. I did not want to be faced with confronting the reality I was trying so hard to avoid. I didn't know what to do but I knew that we both had to get through it. I was learning to trust God while trying to hold back my own tears.

Even though she tried to keep her emotions from me, I knew when something was wrong. With my mother being ill, I had to truly lean on and trust in God's Word. My mom was unaware of how I felt.

My mom keeps her personal life very private; people didn't know what was going on with her during that time. To protect her privacy, it was hard for me to talk to anyone. I know that not everyone is for me so I leaned on God for help. The scripture that came for my help was Psalms 46:1-3.

Here are some things I learned that may help you:

1. If you have an opportunity to go with your parent to the doctor, don't hesitate to go with them and ask questions. Being present at doctor's appointments will help you understand the disease your parent is battling, and you will get a chance to meet the people who would be instrumental in their treatments.
2. Don't close yourself off to people who want to help you. I say this from experience because I did exactly that and it didn't help at all.
3. Allow God to comfort you and give you peace in the midst of the storm.
4. Tap into your faith and God will give you the strength to have faith over fear.
5. Don't be afraid to talk to your parents, you are not a burden to them. You will not worsen their disease by talking about it. When you talk, you give your parent back some of their humanity that can be lost along the way.
6. Don't let life pass you by, sometimes you may feel selfish if you start doing something fun. When you have a sick parent, try not to feel guilty for living, it will hurt your parent to see you not having fun, sometimes they feel responsible for what happens to you. Just be there along the way throughout their journey.

7. Create a playlist with your parent to help you when you need to sit quietly or meditate. Here is a list of the songs that my mom and I curated:

- "Healing is Here" Deluge
- "Passion" Holy Ground Featuring Melodie Malone
- "Your Spirit" Tasha Cobbs Leaonard
- "Closer" Bethel Music and Steffany Gretzinger
- "You Reign Forever" Psalmist Raine Ministries
- "Your Love" Psalmist Raine
- "A Heart That Forgives" Kevin LaVar
- "Reckless Love" Israel Houghton
- "You Say" Lauren Daigle
- "God Can Do Anything" VaShawn Mitchell
- "Waymaker" Benita Jones took me through the process of going to doctor appointments until the surgery
- "No Longer Slaves" Tasha Cobbs Leonard
- "It is Well" Bethel Music
- "Change Me" Tamela Mann God was ministering to me during my rededication
- "You Know My Name" Tasha Cobbs Leonard
- "Alpha And Omega" Israel and New Breed
- "My Worship is For Real" Bishop Larry Trotter

APPENDIX 2

AFFIRMATIONS FROM GOD'S WORD FOR YOUR JOURNEY

Here are a few of my personal favorite scriptures that may bless you as they were a blessing to me throughout my journey. Write the scriptures in your journal along with some of your favorite affirmations to keep your mind stayed on God.

- Proverbs 17:17
- Ephesians 2:8-9
- John 2:19
- John 8:12
- I John 1:7
- Isaiah 55:9
- Proverbs 3:5-6
- Psalms 119:105
- Isaiah 41:10
- Psalm 18:39
- Job 19:13-14
- I John 4:18
- Galatians 6:2
- Matthew 28:20
- John 14:27
- Matthew 17:20
- I Thessalonians 4:13-18
- Jeremiah 29:11
- Isaiah 61:3
- Proverbs 27:17
- I Peter 5:7
- Isaiah 40:29-31
- Joshua 1:9
- Ephesians 3:20-21

- James 2:17
- Philippians 1:6
- Luke 1:37
- Exodus 14:14
- II Kings 20:5
- I John 1:7
- Proverbs 3:5-6
- Isaiah 55:9

APPENDIX 3

CANCER SUPPORT RESOURCES

Compiled by:
LeAnnette Magba-Kamara, RN, BSN

A friend is always loyal, and a brother is born to help in time of need.

Proverbs 17:17 (NLT)

Dear Precious Sister-friends and Caregivers,

Someone once tried to encourage me by saying, "God gives the hardest battles to His strongest soldiers." Looking back, I have to admit that even the strongest soldiers get weak and need a helping hand. As a hospice nurse, I have seen people in all phases of their cancer journey, and I want you to know that I have seen God give them everything they needed when they trusted Him.

Support For Caregivers

It takes a special anointing and strength to walk with someone through the difficulties of their cancer journey. As a caregiver, you answer the call to be a listening ear and a shoulder to cry on. You ensure that your loved one does not walk alone.

As a caregiver, you lend a helping hand to your cancer warrior. When your loved one got the diagnosis and you had to hold your tears in to be "strong for them," God saw those tears. When your breath was taken away and you offered instead a quiet presence or just held their hand because you had no words; God steadied your hand and uplifted your heart.

When your sleepless nights with your loved one morphed into weary days, you found the strength to continue on the journey beside them, loving on them and hoping with them. God heard your prayers of healing and will continue to bless your efforts. As a caregiver, you get a front seat to witness the miraculous wonders God works in the lives of our cancer survivors.

The journey of faith over fear is not just for your cancer survivor. It's also your journey of faith. The enemy will try to plant seeds of doubt in your mind to snatch away the hope of healing. In the quiet of the night, he will whisper that things look hopeless or that the pain is too great, or the journey is too hard to continue supporting them. The enemy is the father of lies! God will give you both what you need.

Resources For Patients/Caregivers

Cancer Family Care, Inc. (Cincinnati)

Local Ohio center offering support for caregivers and patients.

American Cancer Society

Cancer Caregiver Resource Guide
https://www.cancer.org/cancer/caregivers/caregiver-resource-guide.html
A downloadable guide or online tool for those caring for someone with cancer. It can assist with selfcare for the caregiver; steps to help protect your health and well-being, creating a better understanding of what your loved one is going through, and development of skills for coping and caring.

Cancer Hope Network

1-877-467-3638
Free/confidential, personal volunteer telephone support for individuals, and their loved ones, dealing with cancer.

CaringBridge

caringbridge.org

American Cancer Society partners with CaringBridge which is a free online tool for cancer patients, their caregivers, friends and family. CareBridge allows cancer patients and those involved in their care to get help and support. The tool allows the cancer patient and their support network to share the journey with one another and receive health updates.

The Wellness Community and Gilda's Club-Cancer Support Community

1-888-793-9355
Professional Social Work services, education, and free support for all people affected by cancer.

CancerCare
1-800-813-4673
Provides free professional support services either online, via telephone or in-person for caregivers and
loved ones. Additional caregiver resources are available.

Cancer Family Care, Inc. (Cincinnati)
Offers support for caregivers, and patients.

The American Cancer Society
www.Cancer.org/cancer
Offers support for cancer patients and caregivers.

"Unless you people see signs and wonders,"
Jesus told him,
"You will never believe."

John 4:48

ACKNOWLEDGEMENTS

LaKeisha Hawthrone

Nikki Howell

LeAnnette Magba-Kamara

Jewel Presley

Harriett Anderson Burroughs

Ebony Monique

Shantee Boggs

Pastor David & Lady Kelsey Harding

JaQuan Postell

My beautiful granddaughters, **Alaya** and **Amina**, I dedicate this book to you and I pray that it will be a guide in your life as you grow into women that will have faith over fear.

No matter what life may bring you, always open this book and remember that you can do all things through Christ that strengthens you (Philippians 4:11-13). Here is something to remind yourself when times in your life get a little hard:

Today I dare to struggle. Today I dare to win.

When fear knocks, let faith answer the door. 1 John 4:18 There is no fear in love, but perfect love casts out fear. Having faith in God over fear means trusting in God's plan and provision, even in the face of uncertainty, difficulty, or danger. This is my prayer for you:

Heavenly Father,

I lift my granddaughter's faith unto You. In a world that sometimes shakes our beliefs, I pray that Alaya and Amina hold onto their faith with unwavering conviction. May they trust in Your divine plan and find solace in Your everlasting love. Let them not drift from you, and your Word. Let them be confident in Your grace and become the women of God you have called them to be.

Let the reality of your Life, Death and Resurrection be at the forefront of their minds each day in the name of Jesus. Amen.

NiNi loves you with all my heart. (May 2024)

www.ingramcontent.com/pod-product-compliance
Lightning Source LLC
Chambersburg PA
CBHW071145090426
42736CB00012B/2235